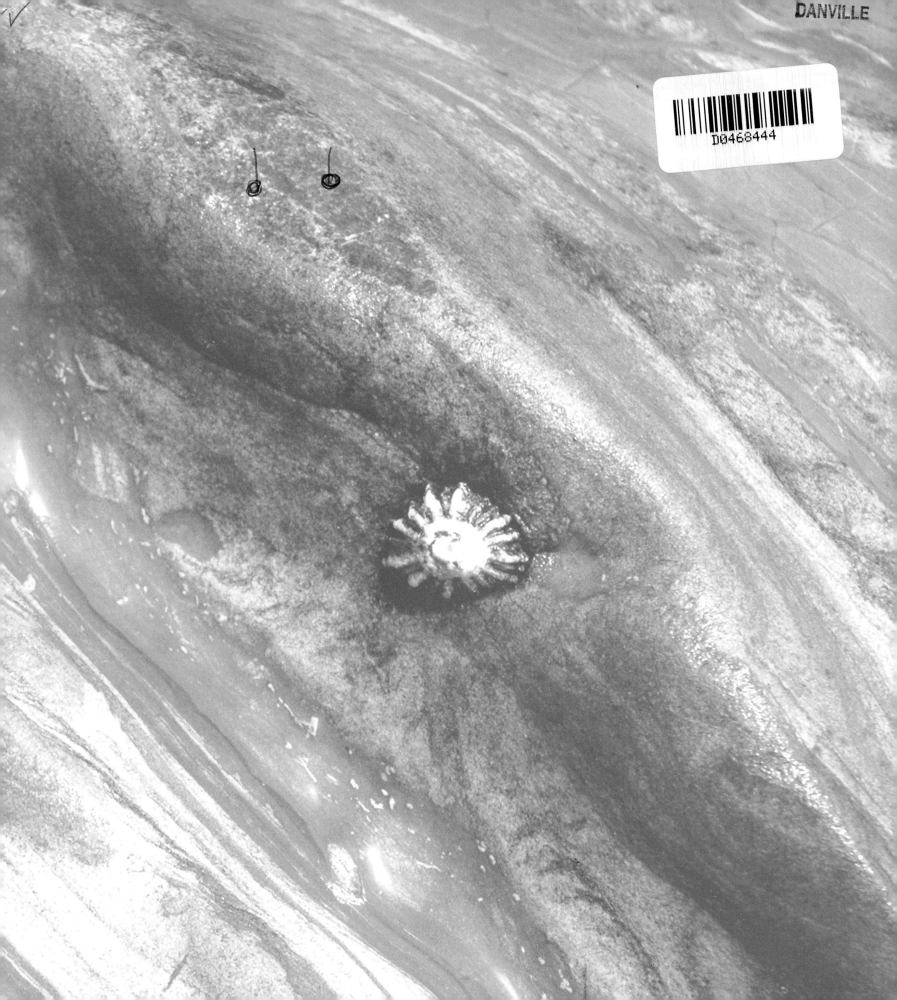

SNAPSHOTS
the wonders of MONTEREY BAY

Words and Pictures by
CELESTE DAVIDSON MANNIS

VIKING

Come with me to the edge of the sea.

Picture a bay where giants play

WHERE THE PACIFIC OCEAN meets centra[l]
California, Monterey Bay yawns wide from Poir[t]
Santa Cruz in the north to Point Piños in the south
The bay harbors more than thirty types of marin[e]
mammals: warm-blooded sea creatures tha[t]
breathe air, nurse their young, and have some hai[r]
Among these are many cetaceans: whales, por[-]
poises, and dolphins. The humpback whale, with it[s]
knobby dorsal fin and barnacle-encrusted fluke, i[s]
a baleen whale, as are blue, gray, and mink[e]
whales. These whales feast on krill, tiny shrimplik[e]
animals, by straining them with baleen: bristly
hairlike plates that hang from their massive jaws.

Sperm whales, orcas, and beaked whale[s]
are toothed whales. Aggressive hunters, they
grasp fish and marine mammals with their teeth
and swallow them whole or in large chunks. Por[-]
poises and dolphins, also considered toothed
whales, eat fish and squid.

And breakers thunder.

STRONG WINDS SWEEP ACROSS the surface of the bay to create powerful waves that travel for miles. These waves hammer the coast, sculpting granite and Santa Cruz mudstone into jagged shards of rocky shoreline and smooth ribbons of sandy beach.

Carved into the seafloor of the bay is the heart of the fifteen-million-year-old Monterey Canyon: bigger than the Grand Canyon and almost two miles deep in some places. The largest submarine valley along the coast of North America, it extends far beyond the boundaries of Monterey Bay. Countless marine animals, from minuscule bone-eating worms to truck-long great white sharks, roam its mysterious depths.

Where a forest floats,

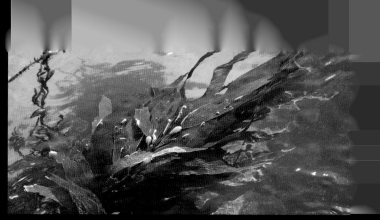

BENEATH THE WAVES, giant kelp thrive in one of the world's largest kelp forests. A single giant kelp can grow up to 100 feet tall and shelter more than 500,000 sea creatures from dozens of species. On the surface, sea otters wrap their young in the slick, floating fronds of the kelp forest's canopy to keep the pups in one spot while they hunt for food.

Sea urchins eat kelp, and otters eat sea urchins. Whole kelp forests have disappeared in areas abandoned by sea otters. That makes sea otters a keystone species: a specific type of animal that is vitally important to the survival of an ecosystem.

And pirates plunder.

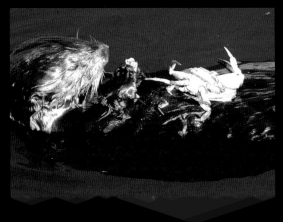

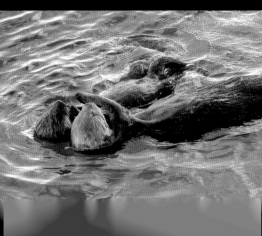

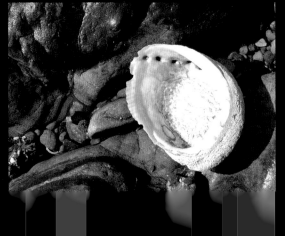

WHETHER DIVING FOR TASTY TREASURES IN A KELP BED, or bobbing on the jewel-bright surface of an emerald cove, sea otters are one of the most fascinating residents of Monterey Bay. As clever as they are cute, these small marine mammals float on their backs and crack shellfish such as crab and abalone with rocks. This makes them one of the few animals other than humans to use tools.

One hundred years ago, sea otters were almost hunted to extinction for their soft, dense furs. Now over two thousand of these lively creatures live in or near Monterey Bay.

Picture a tidepool, rocky and quiet,

THE SHAPE OF THE MONTEREY BAY SHORELINE CHANGES constantly with the ebb and flow of tides: the rising and falling of the water level at different times of day. Intertidal zones are areas of shoreline covered by water at high tide and exposed to air during low tide. Shallow pools of water collect in rocky hollows at low tide to form tidepools.

The bay's tidepools are a dynamic habitat. When the tide ebbs out to sea, tidepools appear still and serene. When the tide flows in to shore, they are lashed by waves. Only the hardiest, most versatile creatures can survive in this environment. Mollusks—soft-bodied creatures with protective shells—and inver-

A sunbathing sea star,

SEA STARS, ANEMONES, AND HERMIT CRABS

are common tidepool invertebrates. Sea stars also known as starfish, grab at rocks with tiny suction cups to keep from being jostled by waves Flowerlike aggregating anemones coat themselves with shells and sand to keep moist, while hermit crabs create homes out of discarded snai shells and carry them wherever they go.

Mollusks have also adapted well to the harsh tidepool environment. To keep moist at low tide rough limpets carve shallow "swimming pools" into rocks with the rough edge of their shells Clusters of California mussels glue themselves to rocks so waves won't wash them away.

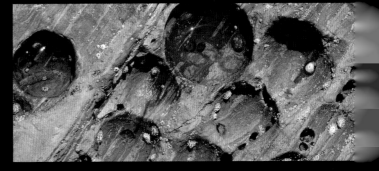

A pinniped riot!

JUST OFFSHORE, FIVE DIFFERENT TYPES

of pinnipeds—marine mammals with flippers—play in Monterey Bay. California sea lions are year-round residents of the bay, while northern fur seals, northern elephant seals, and Steller's sea lions are part-time residents. California sea lions, with their protruding outer ears, sleek dark coats, and loud bark, are hard to miss as they sunbathe in harbors and breakwaters along the coast. Harbor seals, with their speckled coats, prefer to rest on rocky outcroppings at low tide.

Pinniped means "feather-footed" in Latin, and the distinctive flipper "feet" of these intelligent, playful animals do look a bit like feathers. Flippers allow pinnipeds to swim gracefully through the bay, and to climb out onto beaches, rocks, and dunes to rest and have babies.

Picture a dune, ancient and harsh,

MASSIVE SAND HILLS CROWN MANY MONTEREY BAY BEACHES, forming one of the largest dune systems in California. Dunes are created over a long period of time: Those of Monterey Bay took thousands of years to develop. Sand is pushed ashore by waves and carried farther inland by the wind. As the sand accumulates in mounds around driftwood, kelp, and other beach debris, plants such as lupine, strawberry, and beach grass take root and anchor dunes to the beach. Foredunes, those closest to the sea, are a harsh

A secret lair,

FARTHER INLAND, DUNES PROVIDE A sheltered environment where all sorts of animals and plants thrive. A unique habitat for rare moths and butterflies, such as the Smith's blue butterfly, the dunes are also a home to black-tailed and mule deer, the California ground squirrel, and the black legless lizard. The snowy plover, a threatened variety of shorebird, prefers to breed on the dunes of Monterey Bay, while the Menzies wallflower, with its tiny yellow buds, rarely grows anywhere else.

Just north of the bay, the dunes of Año Nuevo provide a rookery for elephant seals, who return to the same beaches year after year to breed. Once pups are born, their mothers nurse them for about a month, until they are old enough to care for themselves.

A welcoming marsh.

ELKHORN SLOUGH (pronounced "slew") is a body of water that extends seven miles inland and flows out into Monterey Bay. The slough is an estuary, a combination of freshwater and saltwater habitats. Surrounded by mudflats, it serves as a nursery for over eighty species of fish, and a refuge for harbor seals, which are hunted relentlessly by great white sharks in the open water. More than 200 types of birds, including the great egret, blue heron, and double-crested cormorant live there, while hundreds more visit it during their annual migration. Pickings are lush for these birds, who dine on fish and over 400 resident species of invertebrates and mollusks.

Picture a tasty fresh seafood buffet,

DURING SPRING AND SUMMER, the surface of the bay is battered by strong offshore winds that push aside the warmer water of the ocean's surface and cause an upwelling of cool water from the depths of the Monterey Canyon. Tiny plants and animals called plankton float to the ocean's surface, providing a feast for large creatures such as krill, fish, and squid. In turn, these animals become food for marine mammals, large fish, and seabirds such as western gulls, shearwaters, and the endangered brown pelican.

Seabirds are uniquely suited for life on the ocean. Able to drink seawater, they also have powerful wings that act like flippers when they dive for fish, and most have feathers that repel water. The brown pelican's bill can expand to hold almost three gallons of fish and water.

And sun's bedtime kiss,
at the end of the day.

BROAD, WHITE SAND BEACHES, TINY POCKET BEACHES, and other beaches that come and go with the seasons, flank more than half the bay's shoreline. Polychaete worms, sand crabs, and ghost shrimp are just a few of the creatures who live burrowed into the sandy shore of the bay. Shorebirds such as the curlew, sandpiper, and black oystercatcher are perfectly adapted to this sandy shore habitat, with long legs ideal for wading in the surf, and beaks tailor-made to scoop, dig, and pry open shells. Lovely to look at and play on, the ever-changing contours of the beach don't seem like a rich habitat for wildlife, but just like the rest of Monterey Bay, they are.

Picture the wonders of Monterey Bay!

Author's Note

WHEN I VISITED MONTEREY BAY FOR THE FIRST TIME, AS A YOUNG CHILD, I was enchanted by its beauty. The sky was bluer, the coast more rugged, and the wildlife a little wilder than anything I'd ever imagined. I was convinced it was pure magic. I still am.

The bay lies at the heart of the Monterey Bay Marine Sanctuary, the largest federally protected marine environment in North America. The sanctuary extends from San Francisco Bay in the north to Cambria in the south, covering over 5,300 square miles of open ocean and 276 miles of shoreline. Within the sanctuary, animals and the environment are studied by scientists, protected by government agencies, and enjoyed by the public. It is truly a national treasure.

Monterey Bay, and coastal areas everywhere, are yours to enjoy. They are also yours to protect. It's very easy to do. Be careful where you walk (stay on shoreline paths where indicated), pick up litter, and don't touch, feed, or disturb wildlife. *Take a snapshot instead!*

I now visit Monterey Bay with my husband and children, and a new generation has fallen under its spell. As we hike and play along the coast, life teems all around us, and we feel a sense of peace we find nowhere else. I like to think the bay has become our sanctuary, as well.

Acknowledgments

Special thanks to Karen Jeffries, public relations writer/coordinator for the Monterey Bay Aquarium, for reviewing this manuscript. Additional thanks to curator Mark Faulkner, also of the aquarium, and ecologist Lorrie Madison of Asilomar State Beach for assistance in the identification of plants and animals in photographs. Lastly, heartfelt gratitude to Robert and Paula for the generous gift of their children Alex, Andrew, and Nastasia, who grace the pages of this book.

ADDITIONAL PHOTO CREDITS: Alyssa Mannis: pp. 4–5, all whale photographs; p. 17, California sea lions on buoy

Key

JACKET FRONT: a lone harbor seal

JACKET BACK: TOP LEFT: baby sea otter wrapped in canopy of giant kelp; TOP RIGHT: gulls descend on fishing boat; BOTTOM LEFT: pink sand verbena on dunes; BOTTOM RIGHT: California sea lions nap on deck

TITLE PAGE: Point Lobos

PP. 2—3: view across cove to headland, Point Lobos

PP. 4—5: MAIN PICTURE: humpback whale fluke; TOP RIGHT: dorsal fins of mother and calf humpback whales; BOTTOM RIGHT: barnacle-encrusted fluke of humpback whale

PP. 6—7: MAIN PICTURE: Point Lobos; BOTTOM LEFT: rocks polished smooth by wave action; BOTTOM CENTER: pocket beach strewn with boulders; BOTTOM RIGHT: offshore rock formation

PP. 8—9: MAIN PICTURE: kelp forest; TOP RIGHT: giant kelp adrift; CENTER RIGHT: giant kelp, leopard shark, and black rockfish, Monterey Bay Aquarium; BOTTOM RIGHT: baby sea otter wrapped in kelp canopy

PP. 10—11: MAIN PICTURE: sea otter eating crab; BOTTOM LEFT: sea otter eating crab; BOTTOM CENTER: sea otter feeding baby; BOTTOM RIGHT: abalone shell

PP. 12—13: MAIN PICTURE: Point Piños, Pacific Grove; BOTTOM LEFT: tidepool ripples; BOTTOM CENTER: giant kelp; BOTTOM RIGHT: juvenile western gull with ochre sea star

PP. 14—15: MAIN PICTURE: ochre sea star and acorn barnacles cling to rock; TOP RIGHT: hermit crab; CENTER RIGHT: rough limpets burrow into rock; BOTTOM RIGHT: aggregating anemones

PP. 16—17: MAIN PICTURE: California sea lions; TOP RIGHT: California sea lions on buoy; BOTTOM RIGHT: harbor seal on rocks

PP. 18—19: MAIN PICTURE: startled birds take flight over sand dunes, Marina State Beach; BOTTOM LEFT: ice plants and bird tracks, Asilomar dunes; BOTTOM CENTER: ice plants and driftwood, Asilomar dunes; BOTTOM RIGHT: lupines

PP. 20—21: MAIN PICTURE: elephant seal pup; TOP RIGHT: black-tailed deer; BOTTOM RIGHT: ground squirrel

PP. 22—23: MAIN PICTURE: great egret; BOTTOM LEFT: bridge over marsh; BOTTOM CENTER: double-crested cormorant; BOTTOM RIGHT: westward view of Elkhorn Slough

PP. 24—25: MAIN PICTURE: brown pelicans, and juvenile and adult western gulls; TOP RIGHT: western gull; BOTTOM RIGHT: brown pelican

PP. 26—27: MAIN PICTURE: Spanish Bay Beach; BOTTOM LEFT: visitors enjoy a walk; BOTTOM CENTER: black oystercatcher; BOTTOM RIGHT: brown pelicans

PP. 28—29: Pebble Beach

Some of the photographs in this book were taken as far north as Point Año Nuevo and as far south as Point Lobos. Just beyond the boundaries of Monterey Bay, these areas are a vital part of the Monterey Bay National Marine Sanctuary ecosystem.

More information on Monterey Bay and the Monterey Bay National Marine Sanctuary is available at your local library and on the following Web sites:

www.montereybayaquarium.com

www.mbnms.nos.noaa.gov (Monterey Bay National Marine Sanctuary)

To my extraordinary family, with oceans of emotion.

VIKING

Published by Penguin Group

Penguin Young Readers Group. 345 Hudson Street.

New York. New York 10014. U.S.A.

Penguin Books Ltd. Registered Offices: 80 Strand, London WC2R 0RL. England

First published in 2006 by Viking, a division of Penguin Young Readers Group

1 3 5 7 9 10 8 6 4 2

Text and photographs copyright © Celeste Davidson Mannis. 2006

LIBRARY OF CONGRESS CATALOGING-IN-PUBLICATION DATA

Mannis. Celeste Davidson.

Snapshots : the wonders of Monterey Bay / words and pictures by Celeste Davidson Mannis.

p. cm.

ISBN 0-670-06062-3 (hardcover)

[1. Marine animals—California—Monterey Bay—Juvenile literature. 2. Monterey Bay (Calif.)—Juvenile literature.] I. Title.

QL164.M35 2006   591.77432—dc22   2005026407

Manufactured in China

Set in Packard and Blue Highway

Book design by Nancy Brennan

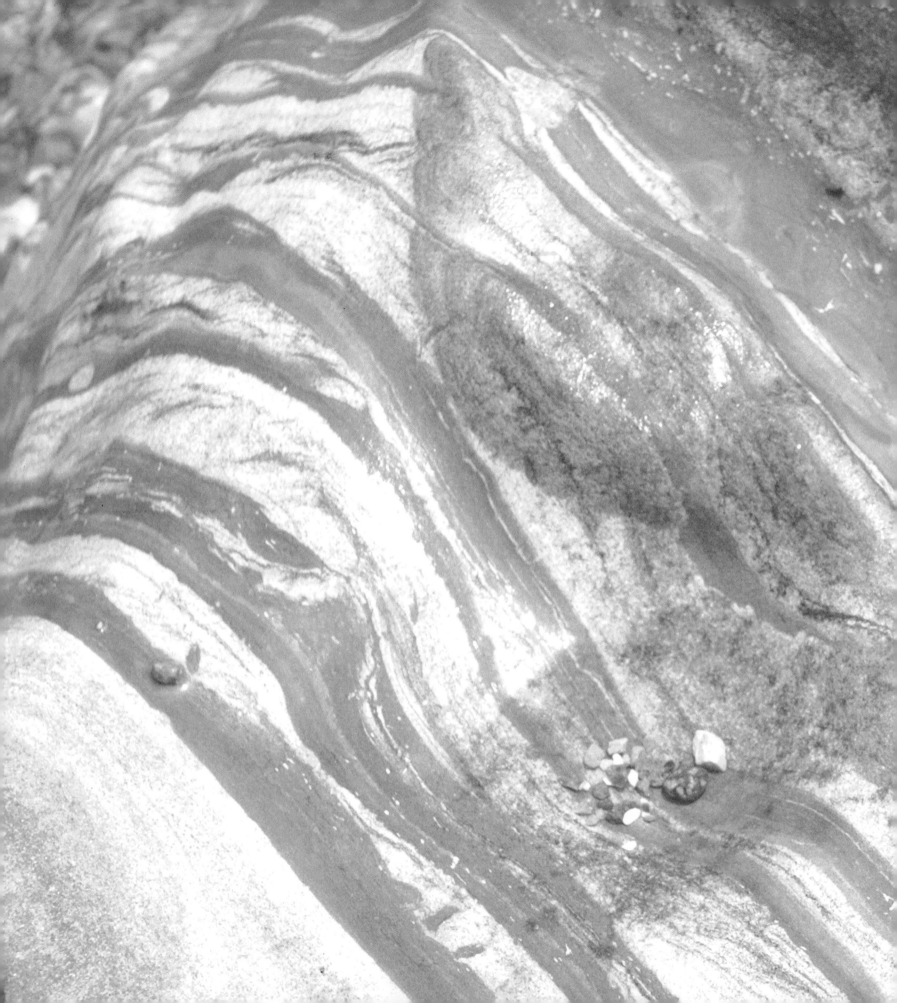